MOUSTACHE

Designed by Roger Lax

Written by Maria Carvainis

New York **quick fox** *London*

Tokyo

To Mousse Repro and The Tigress

Cover art by Roger Lax

In Great Britain: Book Sales Ltd., 78 Newman Street, London W1P 3LA
In Canada: Gage Trade Publishing, P.O. Box 5000, 164 Commander Blvd.,
Agincourt, Ontario M1S 3C7
In Japan: Music Sales Corporation, 4-26-22 Jingumae, Shibuya-ku,
Tokyo 150

We wish to express our thanks to Caswell-Massey Co. & Ltd.; Vincent
Di Prima; Hammacher Schlemmer; Gio Hernandez; Hoffritz for Cutlery,
Inc.;Ian R. Jenkins, M.D.;the Vidal Sassoon organization; Anna Soglow;
Tiffany and Company; Walter Wager, Director of Public Relations,
ASCAP, and, of course, our friends at Quick Fox for their time and
expertise.

–R.L. & M.C.

"The Kiss"

THIS FILM, FEATURING MAY IRWIN AND JOHN C. RISE, SCANDALIZED AUDIENCES IN 1896 FOR ITS REAL-LIFE DEPICTION OF A KISS.

MOUSTACHE

Introduction

The moustache is back and there is no denying it! The increasing number of moustachioed men who populate our lives are evidence of this fact. You merely have to look around you and start counting. Notice that the moustache defies class distinctions as well: newsmen, athletes, artists, construction workers, bankers, policemen, doctors, lawyers are all sporting moustaches.

Why this renaissance of the moustache? It is partly the residue of the 1960s, when hair on the head and on the face became a symbol of protest, nonconformity, and rebellion, clearly encouraged by such popular heroes as the Beatles. In the 1970s, Vidal Sassoon notes that we have moved into a greater refinement of the principles of liberation and freedom. A repertoire of looks has been built to allow you, the individual, to look better and express your individuality. Basically, the moustache is back because of the shared savvy of today's man, who realizes a moustache is an inexpensive, personal way to look better.

People throughout history have placed importance on looking better and have continued to experiment, particularly with their hair, with new ways of doing just that. Obviously, to some extent we all need hair for physical and psychological reasons.

Pogonotrophy, the growing of facial hair, has had a turbulent history. Facial hair has appeared, disappeared, and reappeared with amazing consistency. The Greeks abhorred clean-shaven faces originally and were shocked when Alexander the Great shaved his face. By the time the Romans gained ascendancy, a clean-shaven face was the accepted custom. The Romans viewed facial hair as a sign of the barbarian, slave, or philosopher, the latter staunchly resisting shaving. Toward the end of the Middle Ages and into the Renaissance, short beards and moustaches adorned the most fashionable faces. In the later sixteenth century and throughout the seventeenth century, wigs replaced facial hair as the fashion of the day. Wigs waned by the end of the eighteenth century, but the clean-shaven face persisted as the predominant style. Not until the mid-nineteenth century did facial hair reemerge as a popular fashion.

But unlike earlier periods of popularity, today moustaches are grown for self-expression. In the past the moustache was mandated as fashion by a famous personage or monarch who, in effect, gave men permission to wear a moustache. Vidal Sassoon distinguishes the moustache of the past as a fashion geared to the individual who started the particular style and not to the individual who wore it.

Today the way *you* look is *your* visual message to the outside world. Since no one can duplicate the look you achieve with your moustache, it becomes yet another means of communicating your personal statement to those around you. The individual wears the moustache. In trying to look as good as you possibly can (without going overboard), you moustachioed men have quietly asserted your uniqueness.

The grooming and styling of facial hair is a complicated psychological decision. People invest considerable time and expense in using their appearance to make a statement about themselves, thereby defining their role and interaction with society. Styles often have symbolic meaning, but one should not make conclusive generalizations about an individual based *only* on style. Ultimately one must understand what that style means to the individual.

Facial hair can mean many things: it is often necessary for acceptance and status in a social group; it may signify identification with role models and leaders; or it may symbolically be used to reject the status quo. Military organizations, monastic orders, schools, and other organizations generally control the individual with special grooming requirements such as clean-shaven faces and/or short hair. In the U.S. Army a recruit's face is shaven and his hair is cut off a few hours after his arrival for basic training. Occasionally an example is made of the man with the longest hair by cutting it off in front of the other recruits.

Interpersonal relations are influenced by reactions to facial hair. Psychologists have studied these reactions. In one such study, a group of bearded men began to progressively shave off their beards. They were photographed at each stage: fully bearded, with goatees, with moustaches, and finally clean shaven. People unfamiliar with these men were then asked to evaluate the photographs of each man and describe his personality. Men with facial hair were seen as more masculine, more mature, better looking, more dominant, self-confident, courageous, liberal and industrious.

Psychiatrists and psychologists consider facial hair to be a reflection of conscious and subconscious feelings and motivations. Clinical observation of dream and fantasy material can be of help in understanding these feelings. Dr. Charles Berg reports the following case: a man in psychoanalytic treatment recounted a dream in which he was seated on a bus next to a woman with brilliant red hair. He touched her hair, which gave him pleasure. When the material was analyzed the patient said he did not know anyone with red hair, but then thought of his daughter. He mentioned that recently he had accidentally seen her pubic hair and noticed it was red. This association produced anxiety in the patient, who realized that he might have substituted the sight of his daughter's red pubic hair for the hair on the woman's head. The dream revealed repressed sexual feelings toward the patient's daughter, demonstrating that hair is a powerful sexual symbol.

Freud described the Oedipus complex, in which the child's sexual interest is directed toward the parent of the opposite gender; the sexual fantasies of young children usually involve the parents. The young boy frequently exhibits his penis in front of his mother; however, during adolescence and the onset of puberty, this type of sexual interaction with the mother is not tolerated. The sexual drives are turned elsewhere: either directly toward girls or sublimated into body building, sports competition, cars, and so on. Facial hair, which is a secondary sexual characteristic, develops during this period and may also be used as a way of expressing the sexual drive. Facial hair can sometimes be a subconscious represenation of the penis, and be displayed to the mother and other women in a socially acceptable fashion.

The shape of the moustache may assume specific significance to the man. The classic handlebar might represent the erect phallus, whereas a tiny moustache might represent conflict over displaying sexual drives. Emphasis on grooming and tidiness further express concern with the display of emotions. The excessively neat male may be attempting to control the expression of his sexual emotions, whereas the unkempt male might be demonstrating difficulty controlling his expression.

Shaving off hair also has psychological meaning, as exemplified by the Sampson and Delilah story; Sampson loses his strength when his hair is shaven. Modern-day examples also exist. One man, educated in a restrictive Catholic high school, swore he would never shave after graduation. After ten years of wearing a moustache he decided to shave it off to "see what I was like without it." Once clean shaven, he felt so uncomfortable with himself that he grew the moustache back within a month. He so clearly identified his male adulthood with the moustache that he felt "naked" or vulnerable without it.

During the 1960's, army enlisted men stationed in the United States were required to be clean shaven. An exception was generally made for blacks who wished to wear a small moustache. In Vietnam, however, both whites and blacks, under the intense pressure of war, were permitted to wear moustaches. Reassurance of one's masculinity served as a protective psychological defense against vulnerability to the enemy. A large number of men grew moustaches, many of which were shaved off after returning to civilian life or at the end of the war, when they no longer required psychic support.

Other examples can be cited. One man had undergone a mild depression shortly after the birth of his first child. He later interpreted this depression as secondary to jealous feelings toward his child, who now shared his wife's affections. Approximately five weeks after his child's birth he shaved off his moustache, leaving him with a rather "baby face" appearance, which he later saw as another, more disguised, attempt to deal with jealous feelings and compete for his wife's affections.

Sexual urges, the desire for intimate affectionate relationships, and acceptance by a group are normal psychological needs. Facial hair—its styling and grooming—reflects man's attempts to deal with these normal feelings. The moustache in particular allows a man to remain flexible and comfortable and to express his Self.

IAN ROSS JENKINS, M.D.

The Powerful

At times courageous, at times full of character, wisdom, and dignity, and sometimes

destructive, the statesman, monarch, president, dictator, philosopher, revolutionary, jurist,

PART 1

and soldier is never forgotten for his impact, whether for good or evil, and always remem-

bered for his powerful moustache.

Moustache

Attila KING OF THE HUNS

Kaiser Wilhelm II
KING OF PRUSSIA, LAST HOHENZOLLERN
EMPEROR OF GERMANY

Kaiser Wilhelm I
KING OF PRUSSIA, FIRST HOHENZOLLERN
EMPEROR OF GERMANY

to a pagan chief. Neither wanting to disobey her father nor marry a heathen,

The legendary Saint Modeste, the patron saint of the Slavs, was bethrothed against her will by her father

she prayed for God's intervention. On the day of her wedding, she awoke to discover herself adorned

Archduke Franz Ferdinand with a huge beard!
HIS ASSASSINATION IN 1914 STARTED WORLD WAR I.

Josef V. Stalin
PREMIER, UNION OF SOVIET
SOCIALIST REPUBLICS

V. M. Molotov
SOVIET FOREIGN MINISTER

Martin Luther King, Jr.
AMERICAN CIVIL RIGHTS LEADER

Mohandas Gandhi
LEADER OF THE "FREE INDIA" MOVEMENT

ASSOCIATE JUSTICE, U.S. SUPREME COURT   AMERICAN PHILOSOPHER AND EDUCATOR

Oliver Wendell Holmes, Jr.

John Dewey

Thurgood Marshall

George Santayana

ASSOCIATE JUSTICE, U.S. SUPREME COURT   SPANISH PHILOSOPHER AND POET

Philip IV

Unlike these noble rulers, who established the vogue of a moustache for their
subjects, Peter the Great of Russia de-
creed that a tax of thirty to one hundred
rubles per annum be imposed on any
man who wore a moustache or beard.
Those who could not pay the tax were
given hard labor. Some of those who
shaved off their facial hair feared they
would not be recognized at the gates of
heaven and so preserved their whiskers in
boxes to be buried with them.

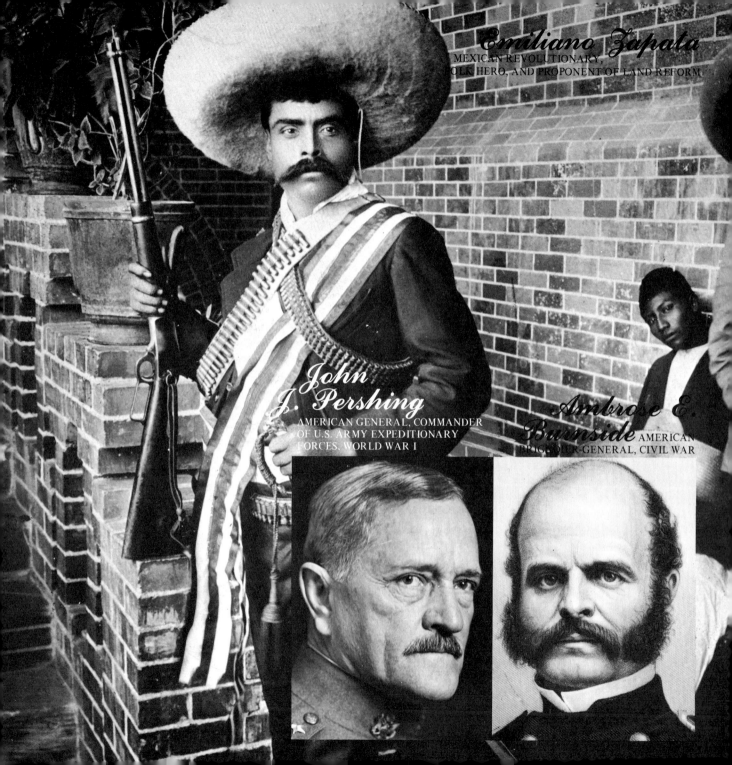

Emiliano Zapata
MEXICAN REVOLUTIONARY,
FOLK HERO, AND PROPONENT OF LAND REFORM

John J. Pershing
AMERICAN GENERAL, COMMANDER
OF U.S. ARMY EXPEDITIONARY
FORCES, WORLD WAR I

Ambrose E. Burnside AMERICAN
BRIGADIER-GENERAL, CIVIL WAR

Charles de Gaulle
FOUNDER AND PRESIDENT OF THE FIFTH REPUBLIC OF FRANCE

Charlemagne
FRANKISH KING AND EMPEROR OF THE WEST

Georges Clemenceau
FRENCH STATESMAN AND PRIME MINISTER

From circa 27 B.C. to 290 A.D. the Gaulish aristocracy was identified by moustaches, while the common people were distinguished by full beards. Charlemagne had a small moustache, short hair, smooth cheeks, and a shaven chin. He insisted, however, on swearing on his beard and forbade any of his descendants from publicly disgracing themselves by appearing with their moustaches shorn.

Albert Schweitzer
BELGIAN HUMANITARIAN

Albert Einstein
AMERICAN PHYSICIST

Seizing upon his porcupinelike upper-lip growth, political observers labeled Dewey "The Moustache" during his 1944 campaign for the presidency.

Thomas E. Dewey
GOVERNOR OF NEW YORK STATE

Anthony Eden
ENGLISH POLITICIAN

Pierre Mendes-France
FRENCH PRIME MINISTER

Clement R. Attlee
BRITISH POLITICIAN AND PRIME MINISTER

Bartolomeo Vanzetti: ANARCHIST WHOSE TRIAL AND EXECUTION FOR MURDER BECAME AN INTERNATIONAL EVENT

When General Gaishi Nagaoka, the father of Japanese aviation, died in 1933, his legendary twenty-inch moustache was interred in a separate mound beside his grave. Such reverence is understandable for Oriental men are, on the whole, less pubigerous than Caucasians.

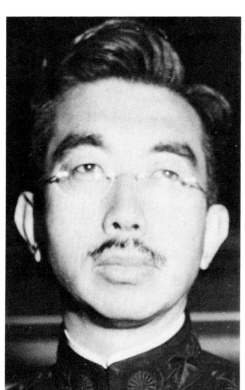

Emperor Hirohito

MONARCH OF JAPAN

Archduke Otto of Hapsburg

PRETENDER TO THE THRONE OF AUSTRIA, 1937

Kemal Ataturk FIRST PRESIDENT OF THE TURKISH REPUBLIC

Mustafa I NINTH EMPEROR OF THE TURKS

Indian Princes

Until the 1850s, the moustache in England was mainly identified with the soldier who had fought in far-off lands of the empire. During the Crimean War, the admiration of the English, especially among the large numbers of volunteers, for their ally, the ferociously foliaged Turks, ended the military monopoly of the moustache. Returning home, Englishmen imported big bushes on their upper lips.
In no time, the rage for the moustache swept throughout the United States as well.

Rana of Poubaudar
INDIAN PRINCE

British army psychiatrist Major Geoffrey Peberdy, studying 400 moustachioed applicants for officer training, classified his subjects accordingly: trimmed, bushy, toothbrush (an example of which is found on this page), hairline, and divided. Noting that not a single toothbrush moustache passed, Peberdy further discovered that the military boards appraised the toothbrush candidate and found them as a rule "too limited in imagination, too little appreciative of the views of others, [liable to] create rather than disperse interpersonal tensions. Like their moustaches, so tended these men: faintly rebellious, energetic but prickly, precise to a fault, disciplining to near ruthlessness and disciplined to near self-mutilation." In a similar study conducted by a fellow psychiatrist, not a single toothbrush moustache passed.

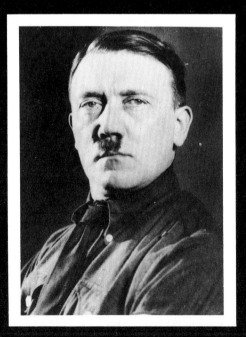

Adolf Hitler
CHANCELLOR AND FÜHRER OF THE THIRD REICH

Prince Otto von Bismarck
IMPERIAL CHANCELLOR OF THE GERMAN EMPIRE

Friedrich Nietzsche
GERMAN PHILOSOPHER

Grover Cleveland

Not since the presidencies of these men has a moustachioed president occupied the White House. The candidacy of Thomas E. Dewey prompted political science students to compile these statistics.*

1. No moustached President ever declared war. 2. Both the enactment and repeal of prohibition was a non-moustached affair. 3. One moustached President married twice.
4. One moustached President was a bachelor when he entered the White House and later married.

5. A moustached President was the youngest Executive in the White House [until John F. Kennedy].
6. America's shortest inaugural address (fifty words) was delivered by a moustached President.
7. A moustached President ran for a third term but was defeated.

*"The Saga of the Moustache", The New York Times, August 20, 1944.

Chester A. Arthur

Theodore Roosevelt

William H. Taft

Theodoric
KING OF THE OSTROGOTHS

King Victor
Emmanuel III
LAST MONARCH OF ITALY

Anwar Sadat
PRESIDENT, UNITED ARAB REPUBLIC

Moslems swear by the beard of the Prophet, Muhammad, who ordained all his followers to grow facial hair as a means to distinguish themselves from Christians, and to trim their facial hair to distinguish themselves from Jews, who wore beards. To many Moslems shaving is still a sacrilege. Until recently the Moabite Arabs viewed shaving as a milder alternative to the death penalty.

Kublai Khan
FOUNDER OF THE MONGOL DYNASTY IN CHINA

PART 2

Regardless of the form through which these artists have expressed themselves, they all understand the value of the symbol for its ability to represent the reality that their imaginations dictate into existence. The musician's and composer's notes, the painter's colors and canvas, the sculptor's materials, the comedian's routine, the actor's portrayal, the writer's language, the photographer's print, the singer's voice, the choreographer's ballet all serve the same need for creative expression. But when each of these artists has wanted to express a personal self, it is not surprising that so many have used a moustache.

The Artistic

*The Moustache Game**

This game can be played by two people or any multiple thereof (possibly teams of two) as they walk down a street, ride the bus, subway, or car. The object of Moustache is to sight more moustaches than your opponent. When either of you sights a moustachioed individual, he or she shouts, "Moustache!"

An individual moustache scores 10 points; a box or triangular moustache scores 20 points; a pencil-line or pointy-waxed moustache scores 30 points; a handlebar moustache scores 50 points; a walrus or Zapata moustache scores 75 points; and a Burnsides or Fu Manchu scores 100 points. A red moustache of any of these styles immediately scores the value of the style plus 100 points. Similarly, a moustachioed woman scores 200 points plus the value of the style, and a red-moustachioed woman scores 500 points plus the value of the style. Neither of these last two possibilities has ever been sighted.

Should the same moustache be sighted simultaneously, the points are shared by the players. If a moustache is sighted which combines two or more styles, the player receives the points for all the styles. Any disputes over the correct classification of styles must be amicably decided between the players, or no points are received. Before you begin play, a time period should be established; the winner is the player with the most points accumulated in that time.

An adaptation of the game of Beaver, invented by British author D.B. Wyndham Lewis.

Moustache

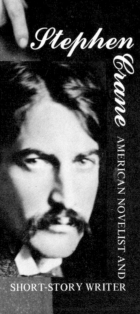

ITALIAN COMPOSER *Puccini*

Giacomo

Louis Calhern

AMERICAN ACTOR

Stephen

Crane

AMERICAN NOVELIST AND

SHORT-STORY WRITER

ENGLISH ACTOR *Ronald Colman*

AMERICAN PLAYWRIGHT *Robert E. Sherwood*

"A kiss without a moustache
is like an egg without salt."
Old Spanish saying.

FRENCH PAINTER *Eugène* ...

OR 1838? ...

John Masefield

Thomas Mann

ENGLISH NOVELIST AND POET LAUREATE

GERMAN NOVELIST

Jacques Thibaud

FRENCH VIOLINIST

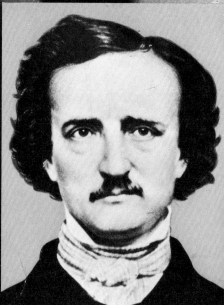

Maxim Gorki

GERMAN POET

AMERICAN POET AND SHORT-STORY WRITER

Rainer Maria Rilke

Edgar Allen Poe

Walt Disney
AMERICAN CARTOON ANIMATOR

Tennessee Ernie Ford
AMERICAN COUNTRY-MUSIC SINGER

Duke Ellington
AMERICAN JAZZ PIANIST AND COMPOSER

George Orwell
ENGLISH NOVELIST

Oliver Hardy AMERICAN COMEDIAN (LEFT) WITH
HIS PARTNER STAN LAUREL.

Girls bat their lashes
For boys with moustaches.
—ROGER LAX

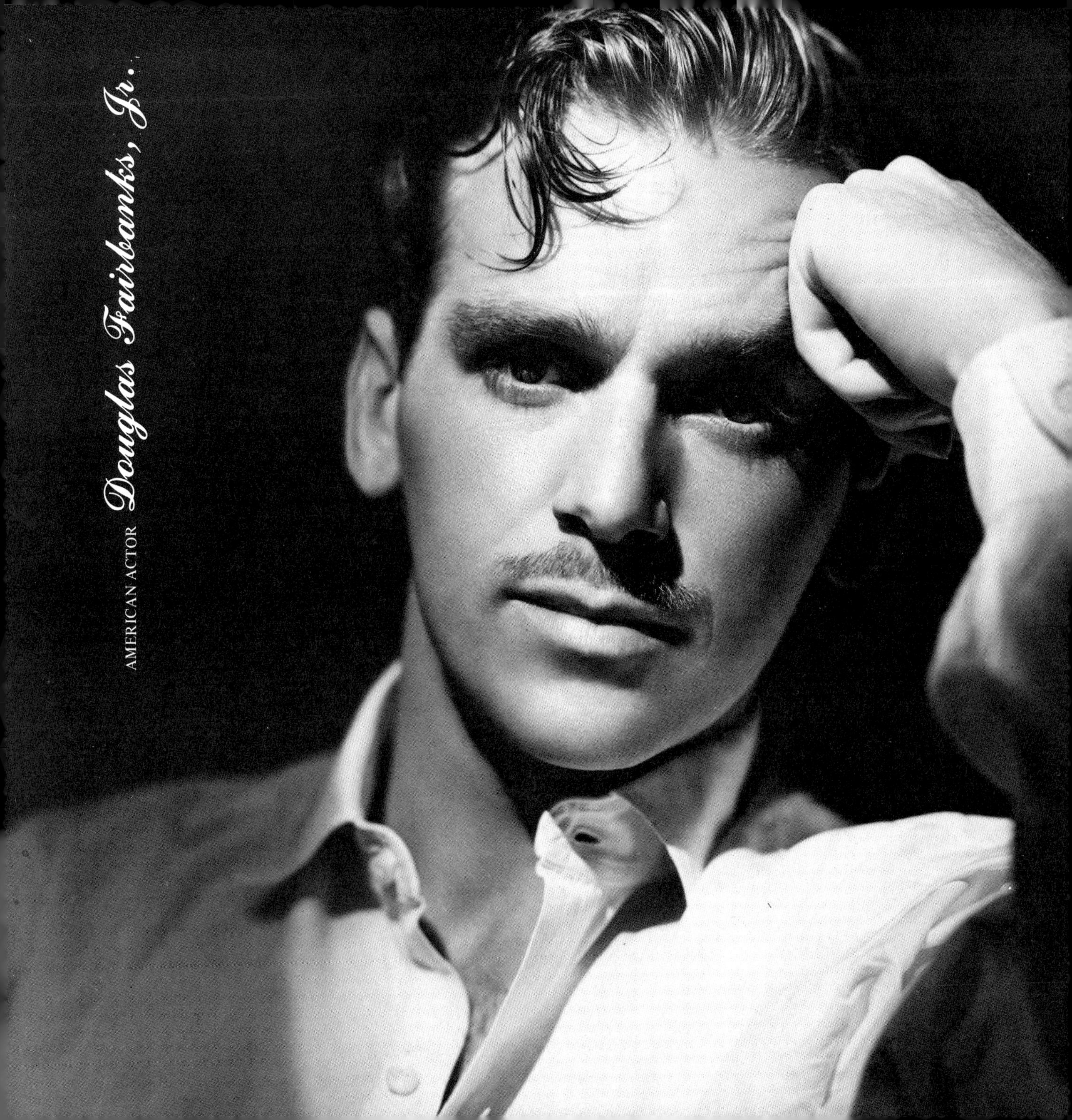

AMERICAN ACTOR *Douglas Fairbanks, Jr.*

Dashiell Hammett
AMERICAN MYSTERY WRITER

Thornton Wilder
AMERICAN PLAYWRIGHT AND NOVELIST

Basil Rathbone
SOUTH AFRICAN ACTOR

Sergei

Diaghilev

RUSSIAN CHOREOGRAPHER

Léon Bakst

RUSSIAN COMPOSER, RUSSIAN CHOREOGRAPHER, AND RUSSIAN SET AND COSTUME DESIGNER FOR THE BALLET RUSSES

Igor Stravinsky, Karsavina, Sergei Diaghilev,

"If it be true that a good face needs no whiskers, 'tis true that a good farce needs no tag—yet to good faces they do use good bushes, and good faces prove the better by the help of good tags."

—Epilogue from *The Moustache Movement*, a popular play written by Robert Barnabas Brough, an Englishman, in 1854

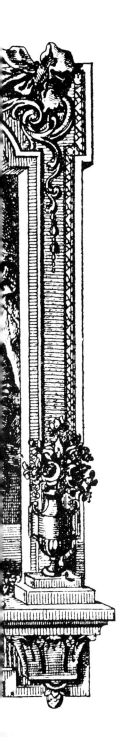

Molière
FRENCH SATIRIST AND PLAYWRIGHT

Eugene O'Neill
AMERICAN PLAYWRIGHT

William Saroyan
AMERICAN PLAYWRIGHT

Tennessee Williams
AMERICAN PLAYWRIGHT

Alexandre
Dumas fils
FRENCH NOVELIST AND PLAYWRIGHT

ENGLISH LIBRETTIST AND POET

ENGLISH COMPOSER

Sir William Gilbert

Sir Arthur S. Sullivan

William Faulkner AMERICAN NOVELIST

Marcel Proust FRENCH NOVELIST

John Steinbeck AMERICAN NOVELIST

Rudyard Kipling ENGLISH NOVELIST

ENGLISH NOVELIST, HISTORIAN, AND SOCIOLOGIST

H. G. Wells

Clark Gable

Vivien Leigh

PORTRAYING RHETT BUTLER AND SCARLETT O'HARA IN *GONE WITH THE WIND*

Art Buchwald's secret for kissing with a moustache: "Rub moustache softly across a woman's cheek, back and forth, grazing so it just touches the skin, causing goose pimples to start from the toes and ascend upward."

Enrico Caruso ITALIAN TENOR

Ford Maddox Ford
ENGLISH NOVELIST

Gordon Parks
AMERICAN PHOTOGRAPHER

E. M. Forster
ENGLISH NOVELIST

D. H. Lawrence
ENGLISH NOVELIST

Joseph von Sternberg
GERMAN FILM DIRECTOR

Xavier Cugat
INTERNATIONAL BANDLEADER

Paul Whiteman
AMERICAN BANDLEADER

Maugham

William Somerset

ENGLISH NOVELIST AND
SHORT-STORY WRITER

Thomas Hardy

ENGLISH NOVELIST

Brett Harte
AMERICAN NOVELIST

O. Henry
AMERICAN SHORT-STORY WRITER

Charlie Chaplin
AMERICAN COMEDIAN

Ernest Hemingway AMERICAN NOVELIST

AMERICAN ACTOR

Adolphe Menjou

Thomas Hope
ENGLISH ANTIQUARIAN AND WRITER

Jimmy Edwards ENGLISH COMEDIAN

Jerry Colonna AMERICAN COMEDIAN

Terry-Thomas ENGLISH COMEDIAN

Arturo Toscanini ITALIAN CONDUCTOR

Igor Stravinsky

RUSSIAN COMPOSER

W. C. Handy

AMERICAN BLUES COMPOSER

Alexander P. Borodin

RUSSIAN COMPOSER

Victor Herbert

NOTED AMERICAN COMPOSER, FOUNDER
OF THE AMERICAN SOCIETY
OF COMPOSERS, AUTHORS
AND PUBLISHERS, 1914

Groucho Marx
AMERICAN COMEDIAN

Robert AMERICAN HUMORIST *Benchley*

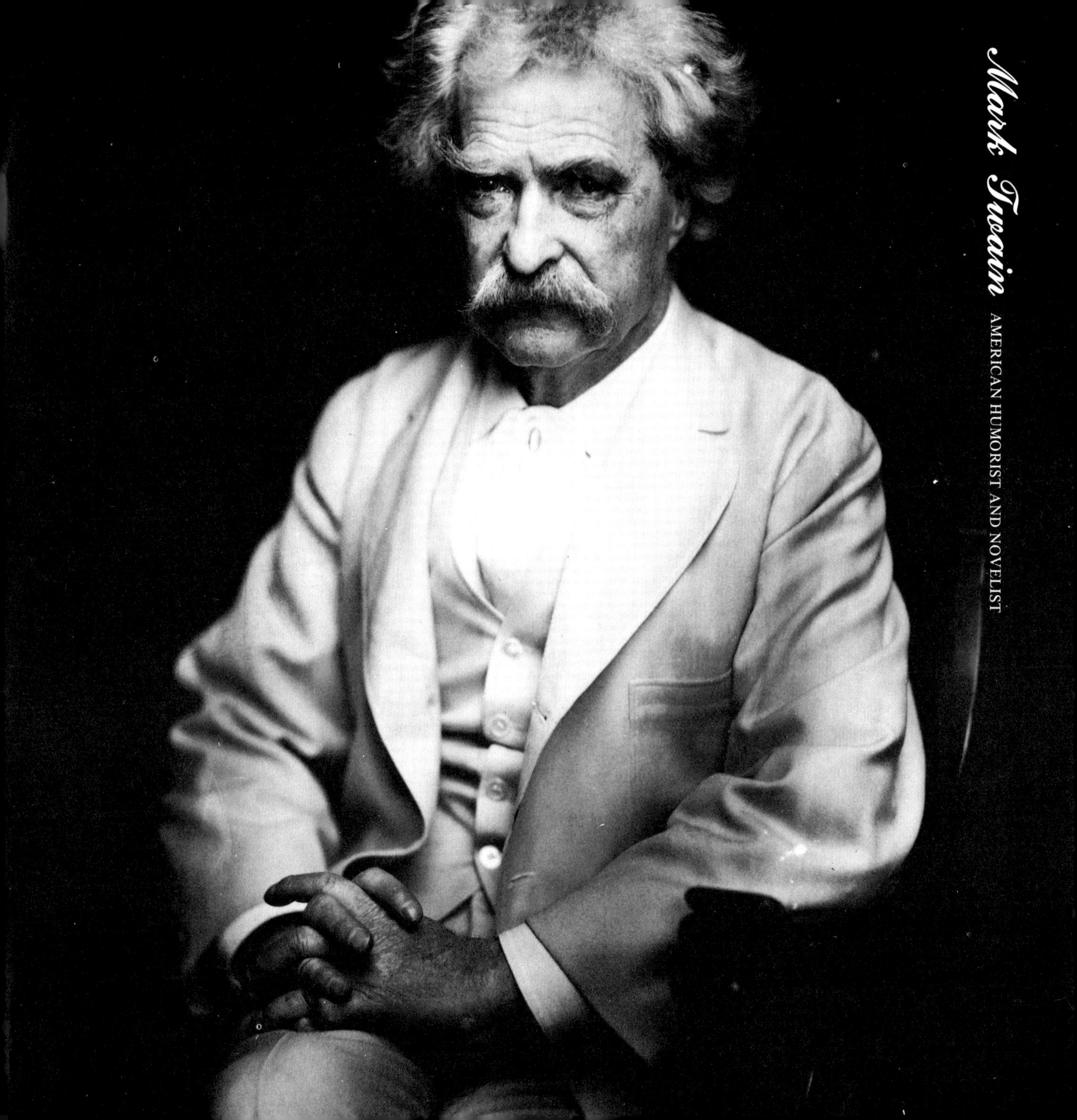

Mark Twain

AMERICAN HUMORIST AND NOVELIST

ILLUSTRATED BY JOHN TENNIEL IN LEWIS CARROLL'S
THROUGH THE LOOKING GLASS

The Fictional

The accepted myth that a man dons a moustache and gains a disguise just doesn't hold up; rather than diverting attention, a moustache accents a man. Certainly this is true of such revered detectives as Hercule Poirot, Inspector Clouseau, Dr. Watson, Philo Vance, and The Thin Man. Cartoonists particularly understand the power of the moustache to highlight their wonderful creations: Mandrake the Magician, Mutt and Jeff, Blimpey, et al. From art to the movies to advertising, the lure of the moustache is felt.

Moustache
PART 3

Major Joppolo and Tina

PORTRAYED BY JOHN HODIAK AND GENE TIERNEY IN *BELL FOR ADANO* BASED ON JOHN HERSHEY'S STORY

El Exigente   *The Crunch Man*   *The Cisco Kid*

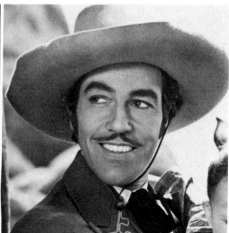

FROM THE SAVARIN COMMERCIAL PORTRAYED BY CARLOS MONTALBAN

FROM THE DORITOS BRAND TORTILLA CHIPS COMMERCIAL PORTRAYED BY AVERY SCHREIBER

PORTRAYED BY CAESAR ROMERO

Citizen
Kane

PORTRAYED BY ORSON WELLES IN *CITIZEN KANE*

Barnaby

PORTRAYED BY RAY BOLGER IN *BABES IN TOYLAND*.
©WALT DISNEY PRODUCTIONS

Blimpey FROM "POPEYE" BY BUD SAGENDORF

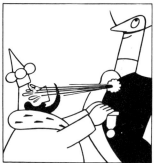

Prince Fizzle FROM "THE LITTLE KING" BY OTTO SOGLOW, ©ANNA SOGLOW

Mutt and Jeff BY AL SMITH

Sgt. Pepper and The Beatles

The Keystone Cops

DUMAS AND MORT WALKER

APPLES ARE NOT ORANGES, AND PLEASURE IS NOT HAPPINESS

RIGHT

BUT I BELIEVE IT WAS NO ACCIDENT. THE HANGMAN'S KNOT IS A SYMBOL OF DEATH!

SOMETHING DOWN THERE IS TRYING TO SEND US A MESSAGE!

TOMORROW: THE DREAM.

Funny Floyd

Mandrake the Magician

Hercule Poirot
PORTRAYED BY ALBERT FINNEY IN *MURDER ON THE ORIENT EXPRESS*
BASED ON AGATHA CHRISTIE'S STORY

Dr. Watson
PORTRAYED BY NIGEL BRUCE

L.H.O.O.Q.

BY MARCEL DUCHAMPS, 1919 PENCIL ON A REPRODUCTION,
PRIVATE   COLLECTION

IF YOU'VE ONLY GOT A MOUSTACHE.

(COMIC SONG.)

Written by GEORGE COOPER.

Composed by STEPHEN C. FOSTER.

Con Esprit.

1. Oh! all of you poor sin - gle men, Don't ev - er give up in des - pair, For there's al - ways a chance while there's life To cap - ture the hearts of the fair, No mat - ter what may be your age, You al - ways may cut a fine

"Got a Moustache"

dash, You will suit all the girls to a hair If you've

on — ly got a mous-tache, A mous-tache, a mous-

tache, If you've on - - - ly got a mous - tache.

2.
No matter for manners or style,
   No matter for birth or for fame,
All these *used* to have something to do
   With young ladies changing their name,
There's no reason now to despond,
   Or go and do any thing rash,
For you'll do though you can't raise a cent,
   If you'll only raise a moustache !
      A moustache, a moustache,
      If you'll only raise a moustache.

3.
Your head may be thick as a block,
   And empty as any foot-ball,
Oh ! your eyes may be green as the grass
   Your heart just as hard as a wall.
Yet take the advice that I give,
   You'll soon gain affection and cash,
And will be all the rage with the girls,
   If you'll only get a moustache,
      A moustache, a moustache,
      If you'll only get a moustache.

4.
I once was in sorrow and tears
   Because I was jilted you know,
So right down to the river I ran
   To quickly dispose of my woe,
A good friend he gave me advice
   And timely prevented the splash,
Now at home I've a wife and ten heirs,
   And all through a handsome moustache,
      A moustache, a moustache,
      And all through a handsome
         moustache.

Entered according to act of Congress in the year 1864, by E. A. Daggett, in the Clerk's office of the U. S. Dist. Court for the Southern Dist. of N York.

© 1862, PUBLISHED POSTHUMOUSLY 1864, WORDS BY GEORGE COOPER, A
FRIEND OF THE COMPOSER, STEPHEN COLLINS FOSTER

Philo Vance and *Hilda Lake*

PORTRAYED BY WILLIAM POWELL AND MARY ASTOR IN *KENNEL MURDER CASE* BASED ON S.S. VAN DINE'S STORY

PORTRAYED BY PETER USTINOV IN *DEATH ON THE NILE* BASED ON AGATHA CHRISTIE'S STORY

Hercule Poirot

Nick Charles *and Asta*

PORTRAYED BY WILLIAM POWELL IN *THE THIN MAN* BASED ON DASHIELL HAMMETT'S STORY

Inspector Jacques Clouseau

PORTRAYED BY PETER SELLERS IN *THE RETURN OF THE PINK PANTHER*

The Occupational

Whether a man works on a baseball field, tennis or basketball court, in a fighter's ring, in the street as a policeman, in front of the camera, in a laboratory, in a hospital, on a battlefield, in a kitchen, a bank, in Congress, or in a circus, all must earn a living. Each of these men has realized the means by which a moustache provides an opportunity for rebellion against the ordinariness of daily life. Whatever one's occupation, a moustache adds a dimension of distinction to the man and his profession.

Moustache

PART 4

Chefs S.S. FRANCE, 1929

The Moustache Cafe in Los Angeles, California came by its name because both of its owners have a moustache. Featured on the menu are a Moustache Crêpe (braised sweetbreads simmered in port wine sauce) and a Moustache Omelette (ham, Swiss cheese, chopped tomatoes, and fresh mushrooms).

THE CITIZENS of NEW YORK to their Brave Police, 1863 July 1871.

OUR POLICE.

ALIAS "BOSTON CHARLIE", 1886

Charles

Mason PICKPOCKET AND BANK ROBBER,

ALIAS "GRAND CENTRAL PETE", 1886

Peter

Lake BANK ROBBER,

William

Johnson PICKPOCKET, 1886

Davey Lopes

AMERICAN BASEBALL PLAYER FOR THE LOS ANGELES DODGERS

"Rollie" Fingers

AMERICAN BASEBALL PLAYER FOR THE SAN DIEGO PADRES

Joe Rudi

AMERICAN BASEBALL PLAYER FOR OAKLAND ATHLETICS

During the 1971-1972 baseball season a moustache was the trademark of the Oakland Athletics, so every player sported a moustache.

Leonard Wood

George Dewey

AMERICAN GENERAL, COMMANDER OF THE FIRST U.S. VOLUNTEER CAVALRY REGIMENT (THE ROUGH RIDERS), SPANISH-AMERICAN WAR

AMERICAN ADMIRAL, COMMANDER OF THE U.S. ASIATIC SQUADRON IN THE PHILIPPINES, SPANISH-AMERICAN WAR

Edith Sessions Tupper, a reporter for the Chicago *Chronicle,* commented in 1901 that "moustaches are not so bad as whiskers. They give a man a soldierly air which is not unpleasant. If a man must wear hair on his face, let it be in this shape. A moustache often covers ugly teeth and lips, thereby proving a boon to mankind."

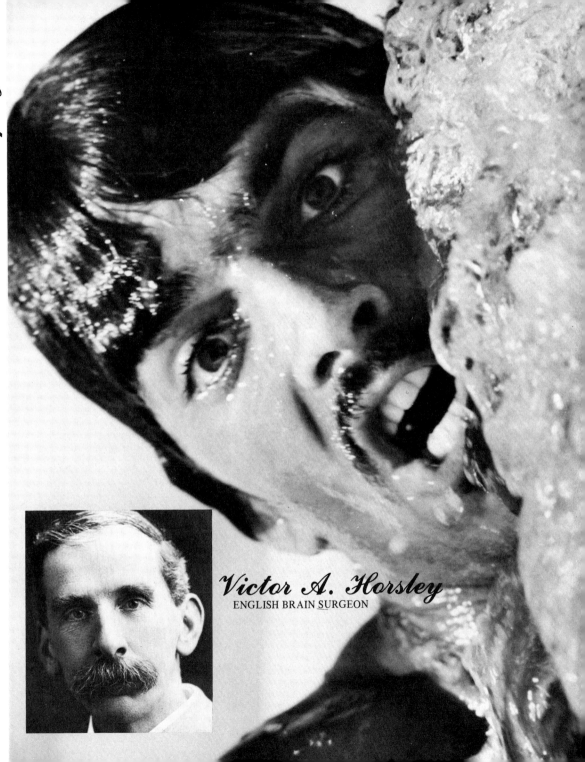

Victor A. Horsley
ENGLISH BRAIN SURGEON

Andrew **W. Mellon**
AMERICAN FINANCIER

Frank **W. Woolworth**
AMERICAN FOUNDER OF
FIVE-AND-DIME CHAIN STORES

Howard **Hughes**
AMERICAN INVENTOR
AND INDUSTRIALIST

Richard W. Sears
RICHARD W. SEARS, FOUNDER AND FIRST PRESIDENT OF SEARS, ROEBUCK AND CO. WITH ALVAH C. ROEBUCK.

AMERICAN FINANCIER AND ART COLLECTOR *Morgan*

John Pierpont

Alvah C. Roebuck

The moustache was at its height in the Gilded Age of the late nineteenth century, when fashion required a moustache and spats. In 1880 sixty percent of the Harvard seniors sported moustaches.

Count Ferdinand von Zeppelin

GERMAN GENERAL, AERONAUT, AND INVENTOR OF THE RIGID DIRIGIBLE

Bailey Greatest Show on Earth

ROTHERS. ABSOLUTELY THE CHAMPIONS IN THEIR SPLENDID AND ORIGINAL LINE OF ACROBATIC PERFORMANCES. CUTING WITH MARVELOUS GRACE, EASE AND PERFECTION EXTRAORDINARY AND INTRICATE FEATS, ON A RAISED PLATFORM.

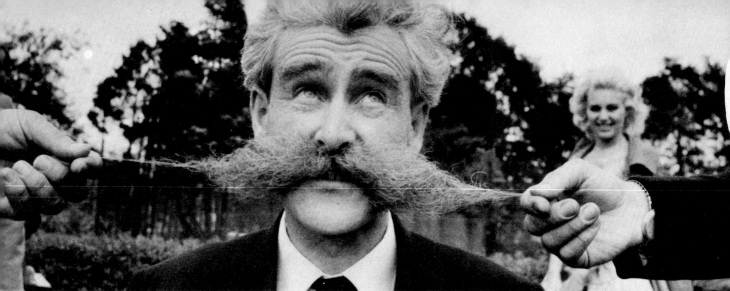

After World War II, the Handlebar Club, along with a number of other groups, was formed to aid those servicemen with hairy upper lips (or beards) in resisting the pressures of civilian life to shave it all off. Paying homage to the handlebar and inspiring others to grow handlebars, the club meets every year to award prizes for the longest handlebar, measured from tip to tip and defined by the club rules as "graspable extremities," and for the prime handlebar, valued for its classic proportions. John Roy, the 1957 champion, measured his handlebar in at nineteen inches.

John Roy and other members of the Handlebar Club

RAF pilots during World War II

During World War II, moustaches, the traditional symbol of the fighting man, sprouted in greater numbers. In England, where the British were keeping a "stiff upper lip" throughout the war, the Royal Air Force went one step further with the sporting of bushy upper lips. So popular was the handlebar within the RAF that it soon became a trademark of this valiant corps.

NORTH POLE EXPLORER

ENGLISH ARCHEOLOGIST,
DISCOVER OF TUTANKHAMEN'S TOMB

Emlyn Baldwin

Howard Carter

BICYCLE PRIZEWINNER IN *"THE EVENING TELEGRAM* CYCLE PARADE", 1893 *Maurice Aron*

AMERICAN ARCHITECT
AND CITY PLANNER

Lewis Mumford

AMERICAN FOOTBALL PLAYER
FOR THE N.Y. GIANTS

Larry Csonka

George Washington Carver AMERICAN AGRICULTURAL CHEMIST

Mike Dillon

AMERICAN SOCCER PLAYER FOR THE WASHINGTON DIPLOMATS. PHOTO © JOHN W. ALBINO, 1978

Mike Dillon had a moustache before this one but shaved it off. He plans to keep this moustache indefinitely because as he says "It's a fancy and I fancy it."

Jim "Catfish" Hunter

AMERICAN BASEBALL PLAYERS FOR THE N.Y. YANKEES

Reggie Jackson

Ron Guidry

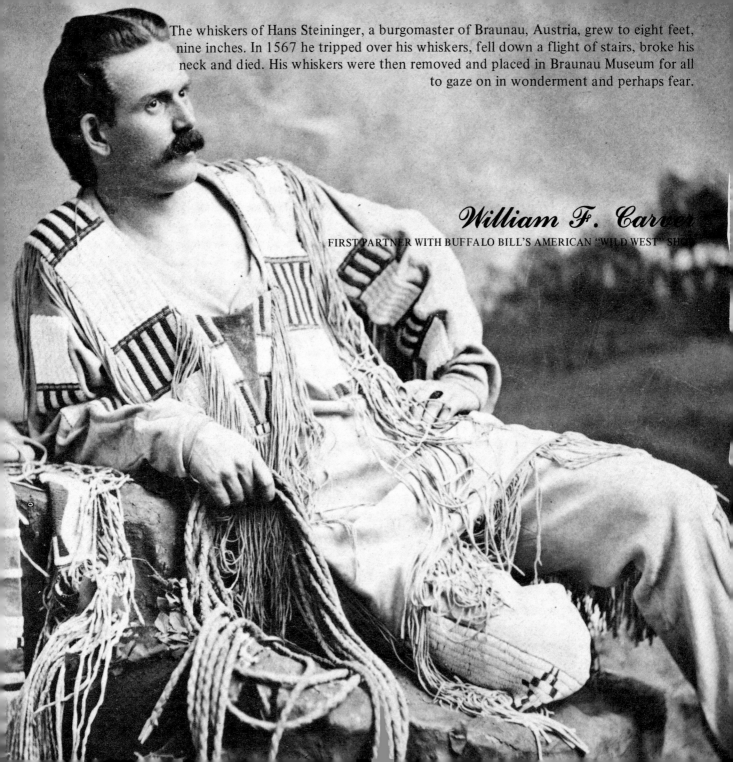

The whiskers of Hans Steininger, a burgomaster of Braunau, Austria, grew to eight feet, nine inches. In 1567 he tripped over his whiskers, fell down a flight of stairs, broke his neck and died. His whiskers were then removed and placed in Braunau Museum for all to gaze on in wonderment and perhaps fear.

William F. Carver
FIRST PARTNER WITH BUFFALO BILL'S AMERICAN "WILD WEST" SHOW

Alexander J. Cassatt

King C. Gillette

PRESIDENT, PENNSYVANIA RAILROAD, 1902

INVENTOR OF THE FIRST SAFETY RAZOR (PATENTED 1904)

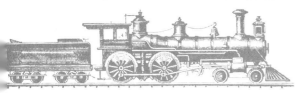

Joe Louis FORMER U.S. HEAVYWEIGHT BOXING CHAMPION

George Foreman

FORMER U.S. HEAVYWEIGHT
CHAMPION OF THE WORLD

John Newcombe AUSTRALIAN TENNIS PLAYER

John Newcombe has had his moustache for
over eight years now and has a stylized
version of it as a business logo.

Butch Cassidy with His Derby Hat Gang

AMERICAN OUTLAW (SEATED RIGHT)

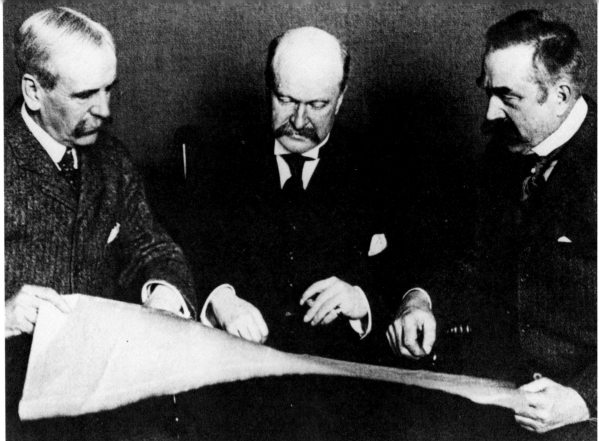

Charles McKim, William Mead, Stanford White

AMERICAN ARCHITECTS

Barbers NEW YORK CITY, 1903

"Bat" Masterson
AMERICAN SHERIFF OF THE OLD WEST
FASTEST SHOOTING AMERICAN MARSHAL OF THE OLD WEST

Wyatt Earp

John "Doc" Holliday
AMERICAN FIGURE OF THE OLD WEST

Aeriel "THE FLYING MAN"

NBC NEWS REPORTER, FORMER MAYOR OF CLEVELAND, OHIO

Carl B. Stokes

AUSTRIAN PSYCHIATRIST

Alfred Adler

BASEBALL PLAYER FOR BOSTON RED SOX

AMERICAN *Jim Rice*

BRITISH EXPLORER IN AFRICA

Sir Henry Morton Stanley

REPRESENTATIVE FROM PENNSYLVANIA

U.S. *Daniel Flood*

SWISS PSYCHIATRIST *Carl Jung*

In the early 1900s many trolley transfers were illustrated with male faces: a man with a chin beard and a moustache; a man with side whiskers and a moustache; a man with chin portieres; and a man with only a moustache. A conductor would punch the illustration that corresponded to the appearance of the male passenger. No hole was punched if the man was clean-shaven.

Allan A. Kingsbury U.S. ARMY BUGLER

Harrison Grey Fiske AMERICAN THEATRICAL PROMOTER ATTENDING PARTY GIVEN IN HIS HONOR, NEW YORK CITY, 1900

After entering the White House, Abraham Lincoln, an unlikely fashion arbiter, grew his beard on the suggestion of a little girl, Grace Bedell, who thought he would look better with whiskers. Shortly thereafter this popular verse could be heard sung throughout the nation:

"I'll put my trust in Providence
And let my whiskers grow."

AMERICAN FOOTBALL PLAYER

FOR OAKLAND RAIDERS

Ben Davidson

Regimental captains

Clown

Your

Whether it be on the top of the head or underneath the nose, hair is the one substance that is part of us which can be molded to improve the geometry, shape, and the character of one's face, depending on how it's done.

— VIDAL SASSOON

A moustache *is* exceptionally versatile, for it can redirect attention from unflattering facial features and/or accent positive features, thereby creating a different-looking you. Specifically, a moustache can compensate for a weak chin, an irregular face, high or broad cheekbones, thin or thick lips, and a low or receding hairline. "Most men," says Vidal Sassoon, "realize that a moustache is an inexpensive, personal way to look better and consider growing a moustache at one time or another."

Today's fashionable moustache is an individual look, dependent on the natural growth of the hair above your lip in terms of both texture and quantity. For the most part, the fashionable moustache is a thick or full moustache, which is well cultivated (shaped and worked) and well groomed. A stylized moustache, such as a Clark Gable or an Errol Flynn, isn't very much in fashion today (unlike twenty or thirty years ago when a character look was very popular). Nowadays, a stylized moustache is considered an eccentric fashion, although a number of men do wear it.

If you already have your moustache, you have experienced the guesswork of how you will look. But if you are considering a moustache for the first time, the inevitable question arises: "How will I look?" Unfortunately, facial hair has a life of its own, quite independent of the hair on your head. Facial hair is considered a secondary sex characteristic related to the hormonal changes that occur at puberty. Therefore, it is very often different in texture, quantity, and thickness. How your moustache will look will depend to some degree on how thick or thin your moustache grows in, how much of a moustache you can grow, and the difference in texture between your moustache and the hair on your head. You will also discover that your facial hair can be an entirely different color and/or shade from the hair on your head. This can be an attractive asset if handled properly.

You can test how you will look with a moustache in a number of ways. Sassoon suggests that you gather a series of photographs of yourself and pencil in various styles over your upper lip. Gio Hernandez of Bergdorf Goodman's barber shop suggests penciling in different styles right onto your face. Neither will give you a true sense of what your moustache to be will look like—only an idea. The only way to know what kind of moustache you will have is to grow it!

Once you let your facial hair grow above your lips, it will take approximately three weeks before the hair on your upper lip is grown out sufficiently for you to know what kind of moustache you can have and two months before your moustache is fully there. Obviously, growing a moustache involves a desire to experiment and a commitment to endure the transition period between clean-shaven and moustachioed. There is no way to avoid the period of embarrassment, the presence of extended five-o'clock shadow, unless you decide to grow

PART 5

Moustache

your moustache while on vacation. Nonetheless, most men are more than satisfied with the end result.

After at least three weeks of growth on your upper lip, you are ready to assess how you look and what style will make you look your best. You will want to consider the shape and features of your face, your height, your hairstyle, your wardrobe, and your life style, in addition to the texture, quantity, and thickness of your facial hair.

In considering the shape and features of your face, you should be aware that a moustache will usually redirect the balance among your nose, lips, and jaw. Today's fashionable moustache, says Sassoon, will usually shorten the nose and bring out the upper lip.

Gio Hernandez thinks that you should look for contrast in the shape and features of your face, and recommends the following guidelines for analyzing your face. If you have a large nose and thin lips, you would probably do better with a wide moustache, one that fills the width of the upper lip area and the entire length of the upper lip as well. If you have a normal nose and thick lips, you should consider a thinner moustache, one that is trimmed down slightly from the nose and trimmed back to the top of the upper lip, but one that spans the width of the lips. If you have a small nose, you should be careful to keep your moustache on a smaller scale, closer to your face. For thin lips, Hernandez advises you to grow as big a moustache as possible to make your mouth appear larger. If you have thick lips, you can wear almost any style, depending on the kind of growth you have. Remember that the narrower the distance between the lips and the nose, the more advisable it is for you to have as full a moustache as possible.

Most men have relatively wide jaws, and this allows them to carry a full moustache and make a strong statement. A full moustache is also recommended since you have no guarantee, even if you have thick hair on your head, that you will have a thick moustache. Unless your moustache is very thick, you will not be able to achieve an even line across its top. If it is not thick, a fuller moustache will help fill in the spaces that may appear. Also, if you are a blond or redhead, a thicker moustache will compensate for the lightness of your hair. Unless you have an abnormally thick growth, your lighter coloring can make your moustache look more sparse. If you have grown your moustache as full as it can be and it is still not thick enough for you, you should consider having your hairstylist layer your moustache, which can produce a thicker look.

However, if you have a small-boned, elongated face with a narrow jaw, you won't be able to carry a big moustache. Depending on the kind of facial hair you can grow, Sassoon advises you to keep your moustache the full length of your lips, more trimmed and less bushy.

If your face tends toward a round shape, you should keep your moustache the length of

your lips, but not excessively wide. It should not appear as a horizontal band across your face; this would be similar to a fat person wearing stripes around the body. In Sassoon's opinion, a very tight little moustache would make your face look bigger, the opposite of what you want to achieve.

If you have an oval-shaped face, you should have a moustache that covers the full length of your lips, as thick as your facial hair will allow, rather than a fussy, stylized one.

The most common mistake made by moustachioed men is growing hair down the corners of their mouths, which gives them a sinister appearance. Neither Sassoon nor Hernandez recommend this look to their clients. "If men would take away those corners," says Sassoon, "they would open up their entire faces."

Along with the considerations of the shape and features of your face, you will want to think about your height, your hairstyle, your wardrobe, and your life style. Taller men are able to carry more hair on their faces, while a closer-to-the-face, less bushy moustache works better for smaller men. Shorter hair can look very good with a full, bushy moustache or a more trimmed, closer-to-the-face moustache. However, if you have curly hair you will want to have a fuller moustache rather than a thin or small one. If you want a stylized moustache, you should remember that today's natural hairstyles will seldom work. Your hair will have to be more stylized too. With long hair you should balance your look with a moustache that is more trimmed and less full.

Your moustache must also work with the kind of clothes you wear and the life you lead. With casual clothes, a well-tailored, fussy moustache will not work. A fuller, more natural moustache will work. If you tend toward more tailored clothes and a more formal life style, a more trimmed, manicured moustache would be better. Again, you must consider how all these elements contribute toward creating a look that makes you look your best.

Since there are so many individual variables, you would be wise to consult a professional. With the fashionable moustache depending on the natural growth of your hair, a stylist can help shape and work your moustache into *your* individual repertoire. People often do not see their assets or defects clearly, and a good stylist offers the third eye of his or her expertise and experience. After all your stylist does your hair, and your moustache has to work with your hairstyle.

Grooming

Your moustache requires the same care and attention that you devote to the hair on top of your head. Remember, in order for your moustache to be healthy and attractive, shampooing—every day if necessary—with high-quality shampoo is essential. Your moustache should be kept as clean as possible, especially since many people sweat first on their upper lips. If this occurs, your moustache will need additional shampooing.

Along with a good shampoo, a good conditioner, one with moisturizers and proteins, will help keep your moustache more manageable and less bristly. Sassoon, who carries his own line of exclusively designed shampoos and conditioners for all types of hair, particularly recommends a conditioner if your moustache is unruly as a result of excessive shampooing or changes in the environment. You should choose a conditioner based on the needs of your moustache. Shampooing and conditioning will also help prevent dryness and skin irritations.

If you find that your moustache has split ends, the ends must be cut back and your moustache should be conditioned more frequently. If you trim your own moustache, remember that you must used scissors of high-quality steel. Special moustache scissors are available for this purpose. Vidal Sassoon and Gio Hernandez use only moustache scissors for trimming.

When you trim your moustache start at the bottom, trimming toward the apex of your moustache. You may find it helpful to press your finger against the edge of your moustache at the point where you wish to trim it back. This should help you gain a nice smooth even line as you trim. Of course, you can have your moustache professionally trimmed.

Besides trimming the bottom of your moustache, you may want to trim it down from the nostrils. A moustache razor will perform this task nicely.

At some point, you may wish to shave out the hollow above your upper lip. Some men like to keep the hollow covered; others like to shave it out. Sassoon thinks a moustache is easier to maintain if you don't shave the hollow. Whether you keep the hair in the hollow or not, it is a matter of what looks best for you. Both Sassoon and Hernandez use moustache scissors for shaving the hollow. However, they are experts and if you find that you can't successfully shave the hollow with scissors, you may want to use a moustache razor.

It seems to make little difference whether you use a comb or brush to groom your moustache. Special combs and brushes are specifically designed for moustaches. Sassoon feels you can use a regular comb with both fine and wide teeth.

Coloring

When your moustache is full grown you may see some difference in its color from the hair on your head. Often men with brown or black hair will sprout red facial hairs. This can be attractive in its own right. If, however, the difference is not uniform, or if you don't like it, you might consider coloring. Highlighting certain areas of the moustache will emphasize the shape and geometry of your face. While some men do this for themselves with standard commercial dyes, which are quite acceptable, the look must be very natural and usually only a professional stylist can successfully achieve the effect.

Occasionally, some men will have a total absence of color, termed leukotrichia, in one area of the hair. This is not grayness but the lack of sufficient melanin in that particular area. If this should appear on your moustache, you can have the area dyed to match your own color.

Most men who dye their facial hair do so because gray hairs are appearing. Sassoon feels this is unfortunate, since unevenness of color can be very appealing. In Hernandez' experience, bleaching the moustache to balance lighter hairs gained by exposure to the sun is not very popular. However, he says, dyeing gray hair is very popular with many men who wish to look younger. Hernandez has noticed that gray often appears in facial hair before the hair on your head and turns red before turning gray. To keep out the gray, you must dye your moustache once a week if it is very gray, less frequently if only some gray hairs appear. For a white moustache to keep the purity of its color, a rinse twice a week is recommended, particularly if the white hair tends to yellow. Often smoking will cause this to happen.

If you wish to dye or rinse your moustache you can use any commercial product, following the instructions on the package. Of course, since your moustache covers a smaller area, apply proportional amounts.

Waxing

While most men who have moustaches do not wax them, many men still do. If you have a stylized moustache you will probably need some wax. Neither Sassoon, who believes the less on the hair the better, cleaner, and nicer it is, nor Hernandez do any waxing. However, Hernandez does suggest waxing for men who want stiff and long moustaches. Waxing will also help you to curl the ends.

Moustache wax was put to an unusual use during the crew-cut craze of the 1950s. It was used by many college students to bristle their hairs; it could make the hairs stand up as much as an inch and a half.

Classic Moustaches

Handlebar

Popular style of the latter half of the nineteenth century and again in England during World War II. The moustache fills the entire length of the upper lip, thus imitating the handlebar of a bicycle. The ends may be of varying length, often achieved by waxing and twirling.

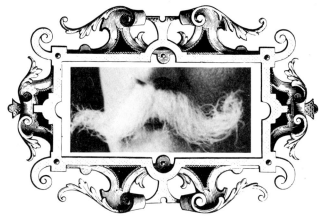

Pencil-line

Popular style of the 1930s and 1940s. This style is, as the name implies, a pencil-thin line across the upper lip, achieved by closely cropping the moustache to the upper lip and trimming the moustache down from the nose and up from the lip.

Burnsides

Inaccurately referred to as mutton chops, this moustache was first worn by Brigadier-General Ambrose E. Burnside during the Civil War. It is full-sized and well-groomed, the ends coming down the sides of the mouth, leading into bushy sidewhiskers. Mutton chops are merely sidewhiskers, very full at the bottom.

The connoisseur's list of fine moustaches is provided below. Some of these styles may be worn in combination, but any such combinations are derivative rather than the pure styles.

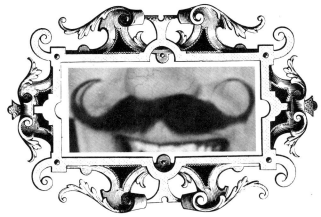

Pointy-waxed

A small-sized moustache that forms, usually toward the outside of the upper lip, into long, spindlelike ends, which extend out by means of waxing to the sides of the face. In the nineteenth century, this moustache was the trademark of the dude or dandy.

Zapata

This style, worn by Emiliano Zapata, the Mexican revolutionary for whom it was named, is a thick, bushy moustache that droops over the upper lip, stopping at the top of the bottom lip, with long thick ends leading off the side of the face.

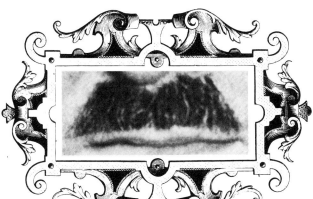

Box

This tight, trimmed-back style has a number of variations, ranging from the abbreviated box to the full trimmed-back version and the sparse box version.

Triangular

As its name implies, this style forms a triangle, the facial hair of the upper lip serving as the sloping sides and the bottom lip serving as the base. This moustache can be worn either bushy or trimmed back, and the moustache may fill the upper lip area fully or in part.

Walrus

This lengthy, full-sized style, probably named for its similarity to the facial hair of the animal of the same name, is a bushy moustache which covers the entire length of the upper lip. It is brushed forward to completely cover the upper lip, usually ending along the top of the bottom lip, although it may cover the entire mouth and extend below. To qualify as a walrus, the bottom line of the moustache must be horizontal, parallel to the floor.

Fu Manchu

This moustache is of Chinese origin and is identifiable by the slender vertical growth of hair from the middle or outer end of the upper lip, progressing downward as far as possible. The emperors of China popularized this style.

CASWELL-MASSEY CO. & LTD.
518 Lexington Avenue
New York, NY 10017
(212) PL 5-2254

Waxes: Pinaud's water-soluble domestic waxes come in tubes and are applied with a combination brush and comb, something like a mascara wand. Available in black, blond, brown, white and chatain (chestnut). Price: $2. These waxes will add some color to your moustache, but the effect is not long-lasting since the wax is water-soluble.

Fixateur, extra fin, manufactured by Gellé Frères, Paris, is another water-soluble wax, highly recommended for its superior quality. Long lasting, subtly fragrant, and colorless, it comes in a stick like a roll-on deodorant and is applied directly to the moustache and combed through the hair with a moustache comb. Price: $3.

Either wax is easily removed by washing with soap and water.

Combs and Brushes: Caswell-Massey sells a plastic moustache comb, manufactured by Speert in Switzerland. Price: $2. Also available is a pure bristle moustache brush and comb set, an exclusive Caswell-Massey item, made in England and designed for a walrus or full-bushed moustache. Price: $8.50.

Razors: A tiny triangular razor, manufactured by Merkur in Germany, is available here. It is ideal for shaving the hollow of the upper lip and trimming around the sides of the moustache. Price: $7.50, including razor and one blade. Additional blades are also available. Price: $1.50 for a package of ten.

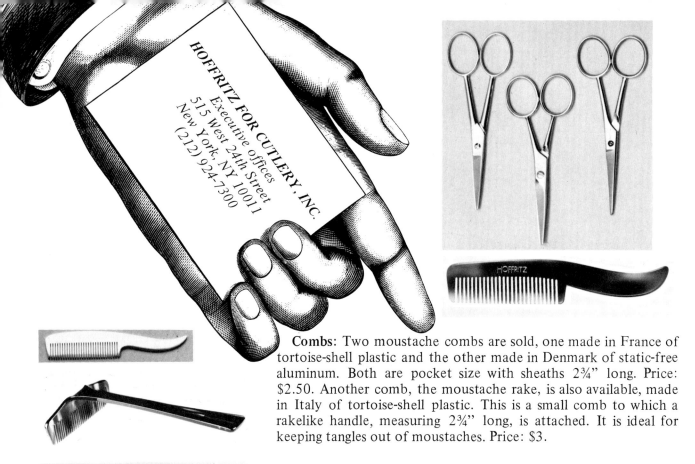

HOFFRITZ FOR CUTLERY, INC.
Executive offices
515 West 24th Street
New York, NY 10011
(212) 924-7300

Combs: Two moustache combs are sold, one made in France of tortoise-shell plastic and the other made in Denmark of static-free aluminum. Both are pocket size with sheaths 2¾" long. Price: $2.50. Another comb, the moustache rake, is also available, made in Italy of tortoise-shell plastic. This is a small comb to which a rakelike handle, measuring 2¾" long, is attached. It is ideal for keeping tangles out of moustaches. Price: $3.

Scissors: Four scissors made of different material and varying in size between 4" to 4½" are available. These scissors have one sharp point and one blunt safety point so that they can be held steady against the skin without cutting it. Small enough for easy handling. The 4½" nickel-plated scissors made in Italy are also available in 4". Price: $10 and $9 respectively. Two other scissors are available: one pair is made in Germany and nickel-plated (4"), and the other is made in France and chrome-plated (4½"). Price: $12 and $19 respectively.

Razors: Two moustache razors are available. Each is 3" long and comes with a tapered head and two cutting edges (one 5/8" and the other 1/4") and a plastic case for easy transportation. One razor is made of chrome and the other is gilt-finished. Price: $9.50 and $13 respectively. Additional blades are also available. Price: $1.25 for a package of ten.

Tiffany carries an elegantly designed moustache comb in 24-carat gold, the ultimate gift for any moustachioed man. Price: $165.

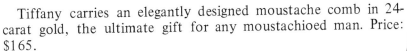

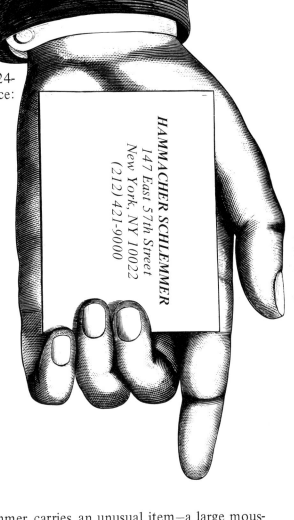

HAMMACHER SCHLEMMER
147 East 57th Street
New York, NY 10022
(212) 421-9000

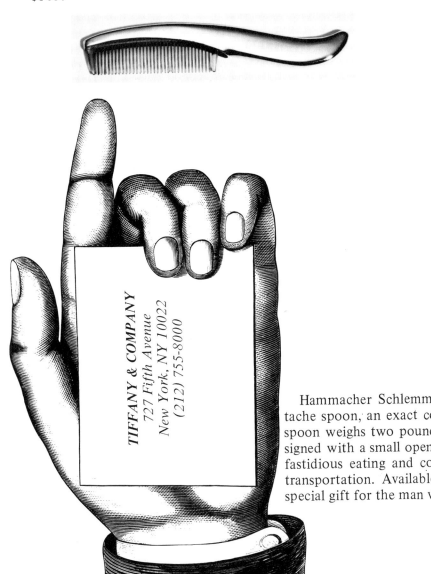

TIFFANY & COMPANY
727 Fifth Avenue
New York, NY 10022
(212) 755-8000

Hammacher Schlemmer carries an unusual item—a large moustache spoon, an exact copy of a nineteenth century original. The spoon weighs two pounds and is 22-carat gold, electroplated. Designed with a small opening in a bridge across the top, it allows for fastidious eating and comes with a red flannel tote bag for easy transportation. Available for both right- and left-handed men. A special gift for the man with a walrus. Price: $15.

Inventions

As fabulous and creative as the classic moustaches were, so too were the wonderful inventions artfully designed to cater to every need of these moustaches. Over forty patents exclusively for moustache equipment were registered with the U.S. Patent Office under such headings as "moustache guards, moustache protectors, moustache trainers, moustache curlers, moustache holders, moustache adjusters, moustache shapers, and moustache bands." Ingeniously made of cloth, wire, clothespinlike devices with springs and clamps, string, and metal, your grandfather was able to preserve and discipline his moustache through the night and sport it proudly during the day.

Of course, the best-known invention to this day is the moustache cup. By means of a "raised lip guard attached to the rim of the cup or a fixed internal ledge attached to one side of the cup," a gentleman could drink tea, coffee, soup, or any other liquid without getting his moustache wet. Designed and manufactured first by Harvey Adams, an Englishman, in 1830 at Longton, Stroke-on-Trent, this item quickly became as necessary to any man with a moustache as the moustache itself. Both right-handed and left-handed cups were designed, the latter more expensive in price, and the sizes of the cups ranged from demitasse to eight ounces to a quart. At first sold individually, the moustache cup was by the end of the nineteenth century sold as a standard piece, accompanied by a matching saucer, in complete sets of china and tableware. Often cups were decorated with landscapes of hunting scenes, birds, people, fruit, and geometrical designs, gilded on both the outside and inside with gold and painted with pastel enamels. Some were inscribed with "Father," "Think of me," and "Love the giver."

Today the most valued of moustache cups are the French ones, those made by the Meissen factory near Dresden, Germany, or the R.S. Prussian cups. Collectors consider Majolica, Imari, Rose Medallion, Sunderland Lustre, and Belleek or cups bearing Crown Derby and Wedgewood marks extremely rare.

Another item, the *schnurbartbinde,* or moustache binder, of German origin, was designed to keep the ends of one's moustache pointed and curled in the fashionable style of Kaiser Wilhelm II. Made of silk gauze, it consisted of two small leather straps and two pieces of plastic webbing. You pressed the binder over your entire moustache and attached it over your head, thereby allowing you to train your moustache at home during the day and keep it disciplined while you slept.

As recently as 1975, another styling device was registered with the U.S. Patent Office by Charles E. Barbarow. His moustache-styling device is designed not only to aid in the selection of an appropriate moustache style, but also to aid in the grooming and maintenance of the style selected. His invention consists of a template attached to a clamp that fits into the mouth. The template can be cut by the user to any desired shape and then held in place above the upper lip for evaluation of the style. Since this device frees one's hands, it also serves as a guide in trimming the moustache to your selected style.

These two inventions appear in the Official Gazette *of the U.S. Patent Office.*

278,999. MUSTACHE-HOLDER. JOHN A. MOORE, Cambridgeport, Mass. Filed Nov. 2, 1882. (No model.)

Claim.—1. In a mustache-holder, the combination, with the comb A, of the spring-prong B, attached to the same and provided with curved arms C, substantially as herein shown and described, and for the purpose set forth.

2. In a mustache-holder, the combination, with the comb A, of the spring-prong B, attached to the same and provided with curved arms C, having cross-pieces D at the ends, substantially as herein shown and described, and for the purpose set forth.

346,831. MUSTACHE-CURLER. JOSEPH B. SULTZER, New York, N. Y. Filed Oct. 28, 1885. (No model.)

Claim.—1. A device for curling mustaches, consisting of a recessed plate and a rotary brush, substantially as described.

2. The combination, in a mustache-curler, of a plate having a recess and a handle and a rotary brush, substantially as described.

3. The combination, in a mustache-curler, of a recessed plate having a pivot-pin with a brush journaled on the pin, substantially as described.

4. The combination, in a mustache-curler, of a recessed plate with a brush detachably journaled thereon, substantially as described.

The moustache styling device invented by Charles E. Barbarow.

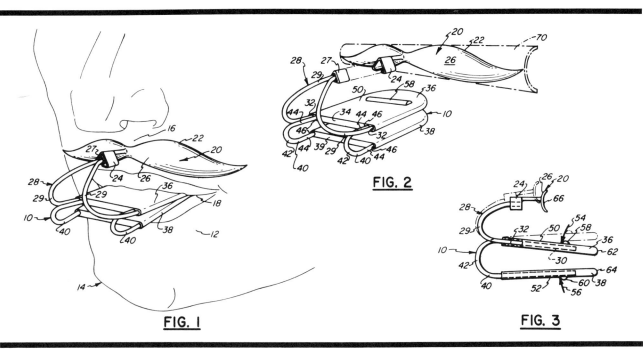

FIG. 1

FIG. 2

FIG. 3

The moustache cups in the background are English in origin and bear Crown Derby marks; the front one is an Imari cup.

Moustache curlers.

Rare left-handed moustache cups and spoon. The cup on the left is silver plate; the one on the right is tin.

Moustache curler with traveling spirit heater.

Permissions and Credits

We wish to express our appreciation to the following sources:

ASCAP: Duke Ellington; W.C. Handy; Victor Herbert; and Tennessee Ernie Ford

Charles E. Barbarow: Moustache styling device

The Bettmann Archive: Aeriel; Athlete; Attila; Barnaby; Howard Carter; Clown; Stephen Crane; Salvador Dalí; Sergei Diaghilev; Alexandre Dumas fils; Douglas Fairbanks, Jr.; Douglas Fairbanks, Sr.; Archduke Franz Ferdinand; Clark Gable and Vivien Leigh; Sir William Gilbert; Maxim Gorki; Dashiell Hammett; Thomas Hardy; Ernest Hemingway; Herbert Brothers; Winslow Homer; Thomas Hope; Victor A. Horsley; Rudyard Kipling; Louis XIV; Thomas Mann; Andrew W. Mellon; Mustafa I; Lewis Mumford; Friedrich Nietzsche; O. Henry; George Orwell; Archduke Otto; John J. Pershing; Philip IV; Walter Pidgeon; Edgar Allan Poe; Marcel Proust; Rainer Maria Rilke; Theodore Roosevelt; Albert Schweitzer; Robert E. Sherwood; Joseph von Sternberg; Igor Stravinsky; Igor Stravinsky, Kasavina, Sergei Diaghilev, Léon Bakst; Sir Arthur S. Sullivan; Theodoric; Jacques Thibaud; Mark Twain; Victor Emmanuel III; The Walrus; Thornton Wilder; Kaiser Wilhelm II; Frank W. Woolworth; and Emiliano Zapata

Boston Red Sox: Jim Rice

Circus World Museum, Baraboo, Wisconsin: The Ringling Brothers

Courtesy of Picture Collection, Cooper-Hewitt Museum Library, Smithsonian Institution, New York: Regimental captains; Allen A. Kingsbury; Indian princes; and Stewart Edward White

Culver Pictures: Kemal Ataturk; Emlyn Baldwin; "Barney Oldfield's Race for Life"; Prince Otto von Bismarck; Alexander P. Borodin; George Washington Carver; William F. Carver; Alexander J. Cassatt; Butch Cassidy; Nick Charles and Asta; The Cisco Kid; Citizen Kane; Inspector Jacques Clouseau; Jerry Colonna; Xavier Cugat; Charles de Gaulle; Eugène Delacroix; George Dewey; John Dewey; Wyatt Earp; Errol Flynn; Ford Maddox Ford; E.M. Forster; The Gatekeeper; King C. Gillette; Oliver Hardy; Brett Hart; Nathaniel Hawthorne; John "Doc" Holliday; Aldous Huxley; Major Joppolo and Tina; The Keystone Cops; Kublai Khan; D.H. Lawrence; Groucho Marx; John Masefield; "Bat" Masterson; William Somerset Maugham; Pierre Mendes-France; Adolphe Menjou; Rana of Poubaudar; Basil Rathbone; George Santayana; Silent screen villains; Sir Henry Morton Stanley; John Steinbeck; Terry-Thomas; Philo Vance and Hilda Lake; Dr. Watson; H.G. Wells; Paul Whiteman; Kaiser Wilhelm I; Alexander Woollcott; and Count Ferdinand von Zeppelin

Jimmy Edwards

Frito Lay Brand Tortilla Chips and Avery Schreiber: The Crunch Man

Hart Pictures Archives: Charlemagne; Molière

King Features, Inc.: Blimpey; Funny Floyd; Mandrake the Magician; Sgt. Pepper and The Beatles; Snuffy